LIVING ON TH

Motorcycle Travels On A Budget

Author: Jacek Klimko

First published: December 2017.

Copyright (C) 2017 by Jacek Klimko

Cover design Copyright (C) 2017 by Jacek Klimko

All rights reserved. No part of this book may be reproduced or used in any manner without the express written permission of the publisher, except for the use of brief quotations in a book review.

Table of content:

Introduction

Entering Iraq

An Assyrian surprise

St Joseph's

The Peacock Angel

Creatures of the night

Kindness without limits

Lost in translation

The oppressed

The refugee crisis

Real nomads

Sleeping rough

Cheap thrills

Moving east

The end of biking season

Forks and tripe

Our half-baked trip to Armenia

In the war zone

Crushed pride

Starting a new chapter

About us

Introduction

Having been on the road for almost a year, we knew the ropes well. Packing, unpacking, pitching a tent, cooking, finding accommodation, etc. - it all became our second nature. By a simple process of elimination, we'd found equilibrium; everything on our bike had its place and purpose. Things we could do without were gone - "use it or lose it" was our motto.

We were gradually learning to deal with the elements. Heat, though tiring, was relatively easy to bear. Cold, on the other hand, together with a strong wind and heavy rain was much harder to endure. Discomfort, to a degree, is a constant companion when travelling on a motorcycle. Though there are ways to improve comfort, it comes at a cost (money, weight, time, safety). I realised that travelling on a motorcycle is an art of compromise.

But the most important lesson we've learned, one that I believe comes only with experience, is that whatever the circumstances, things always work out. Any problem was just an invitation for an unexpected adventure to happen. We learned to have faith in other people, and in our own abilities. That was a priceless lesson.

Entering Iraq

We wouldn't have thought of Iraq as a travel destination, if it wasn't for the stories we'd heard from some of our CouchSurfing guests, who'd hitchhiked through the autonomous Republic of Kurdistan in Northern Iraq. We were told some unbelievable accounts of the hospitality and generosity of Kurdish people, of being invited into strangers' homes, and of being treated like old friends. We wanted to see this place for ourselves, so when the winter was over we left Georgia, drove down through eastern Turkey and found ourselves at the Iraqi border.

It was the beginning of 2014, and even though there was a civil war going on in Iraq and Syria, the Kurdish part of Iraq was safe and peaceful at the time.

The border crossing was just like any other we'd done; militant, dusty and basic. The only difference at first sight was that there seemed to be more machine guns on display than we'd seen anywhere else. For a moment we wondered whether it was a good sign, but at that point it didn't matter; we were going in regardless.

The motorcycle stayed parked outside while we were lead to the customs office to have our entry visas processed. We could tell that the people working there weren't used to seeing foreign tourists like us on a daily basis. Everyone seemed friendly and wanted to talk to us. Some were curious about our travels, others simply wanted to welcome us to the country.

After a short wait, one of the officers waved for us to come forth. At the counter another officer handed us a small stack of paperwork; some for us, some for the motorcycle. A few minutes later we received our Iraq entry stamps. The formal part of the border crossing was over, surprisingly fast.

We'd received 15-day visa-free entry, just as expected, the standard maximum stay at the time. To extend the period blood tests were required. As unbelievable as it sounds, the government apparently decided that it was the best way to keep viruses like HIV out. We didn't fancy a visit to a local hospital, so just thanked them for the 15 days.

Before letting us through, we had to do one more thing; have the motorcycle inspected. It wasn't anything too serious, pretty much just to confirm the number plate, but I suspected that more than anything, the officers wanted to have a nose. I'm sure that asking about the price and maximum speed of the motorcycle was not a part of the standard routine check. Our side panniers quickly drew attention. They were covered in colourful stickers we'd collected during our travels. One of the officers was very disappointed to find that there was no Kurdish flag.

We smiled and promised that we'd get one the first chance we got. That wasn't good enough for him; he called back to the office with some urgency in his voice. When we got there he excitedly pointed his finger at a large Kurdish flag stuck to one of the visa counter windows, and then ever so carefully started peeling it off for us. Moments later, smiling like a Cheshire cat, he handed it over and gestured for us to stick it on one of our panniers. All three of us marched back out to the bike.

Adding the flag to our collection seemed almost like a national ceremony, with the officers and some other people gathering around and cheering in agreement.

Soon the "inspection" was over and we were officially allowed to enter the country. We were in Northern Iraq, more precisely in the Autonomous Republic of Kurdistan, the supposedly safe part of the country.

Almost immediately, I found driving the motorcycle in Kurdistan easy and enjoyable. The road surface was first-class, other drivers were few and far between, and they all seemed to behave very reasonably towards each other and towards us, using their indicators and all. This was a pleasant surprise after all the hair-raising experiences we'd had up in Georgia. Even sign posts here had foreigner-friendly translations. It was all great, but the best thing about driving in Kurdistan was definitely the price of petrol, which was cheaper than water in Europe. With every petrol purchase, came a free bottle of cold water. It might as well have been the other way round; we were paying for the water and it was the petrol that was free.

Coming from Turkey, where petrol is pretty expensive, even by European prices, we entered Iraq driving on fumes. We were hopeful that we'd be able to refill the tank very soon after crossing the border, paying only a fraction of the price we'd been paying up in Turkey.

Not long after crossing the border, petrol stations started appearing everywhere along the dusty road, like mushrooms pushing up through the moist earth on a sunny day. But just like the landscape, the stations were all dry and deserted. None had any petrol. Unsurprisingly, we weren't the only ones wanting to save some money. The demand far exceeded supply. Normally a small price increase would regulate the amount sold, but when we were there, in Kurdistan the petrol market was rigidly controlled by the government and even near the border, where the demand was huge, the prices had to stay exactly the same as everywhere else in Iraq.

Not having any other choice, we drove on, hoping that the bike wouldn't stop in the middle of nowhere. We kept on trying various stations for about thirty miles before eventually hitting the jackpot. Not only did we get to fill the tank, but were also given the chance to rest in a friendly atmosphere. The staff gave us water and some of their snacks to eat. They allowed us to connect to the internet and offered the use of showers. They even told us we could stay overnight if we wanted to rest before continuing our journey, but we had other plans so we thanked them for their generosity and jumped back on the bike.

While still in Turkey, I'd put together a simple route. My research was brief as there was little information available online, especially for bikers, although I did manage to find one useful blog post; a travel account from someone who'd cycled around Kurdistan a few months earlier. The author mentioned a couple of scenic routes and a few towns "worth visiting". Not knowing any better, I held on to that person's advice and wrote down the names of the towns mentioned. One of the places was less than a hundred miles away from the border. That was to be our first stop.

Getting there seemed easy enough on paper. In Iraqi Kurdistan there are two main roads to choose from; one heading straight to the capital city, Erbil, and the other one going in the same direction, but the long way round, through the mountains. That was pretty much it. In these circumstances there seemed no need for a map. I didn't expect to get lost with such a simple choice of two roads, but for some reason, after about an hour I became disoriented. Finding the way proved more complicated than I'd anticipated.

Luckily for us, every half an hour or so there was a military checkpoint manned by armed soldiers, so it was impossible to stray too far and we were soon back on route. They stopped every vehicle, checking documents and occasionally doing random searches. For us, being pulled over was a good chance to ask for directions. Thanks to the soldiers, I quickly found out where to go and knew I wouldn't get lost again.

The soldiers, most of whom were young men, were happy to see us and seemed to be grateful for a short distraction from the boredom of their daily routine. We found it amusing that all of them, without a single exception, wanted to know which football team we supported. It was their favourite subject and a way to place us on their football map of the world.

After a few checkpoints we even learned the names of some of our own national football players. Football definitely connects people, even across cultures, and can be used to strike up a conversation in the most random places. Before leaving home we were both completely clueless when it came to anything football related. It's often claimed that travelling broadens the mind; it sometimes does that in the most peculiar ways.

The final checkpoint before our destination was different from all the others we'd already passed through. For a start, we weren't welcomed with smiles. Quite the opposite, the soldiers were stony-faced and unwelcoming. One of them gestured impatiently for us to move to the side of the road, and with broken English instructed us to get off the motorcycle and show our documents. He then fired an endless string of questions at us, few of which we understood. Truthfully, we told him all about our plans; that we wanted to visit the village and stay there overnight. He didn't like the sound of that, not one little bit, and basically told us to turn around and leave. We knew that if it were up to the soldier, there would be no chance of us going through.

The village was within our reach, just a few miles up the road. Though we were growing tired and impatient after driving in the scorching sun for hours, we saw no other way but to persist, by patiently standing firm and waiting with calm expressions. Having realised that we weren't leaving, he pulled out his phone and called someone of a higher rank to deal with us.

After a long deliberation, they eventually agreed to let us through, but with a strict two-hour deadline. We were warned that under no circumstances could we stay in the village overnight. To enforce this, the soldiers wanted to keep our passports, but that was out of the question. We just played dumb, smiled, stuffed our passports back in our travel pouch and drove on up into the village.

Further down the road we spotted a signpost welcoming us to Iraq proper. Unintentionally, we'd left the Republic of Kurdistan, the part of Iraq from which we knew we shouldn't stray.

An Assyrian surprise

We continued along the road and soon reached Alqosh, our destination. As we drove in, we were a bit baffled to see Christian crosses and Virgin Mary statues everywhere. We soon learned that this small village was one of the oldest Christian settlements in the world, and it all made sense. We'd read a bit about such ancient small Christian villages in Iraq, but now we actually found ourselves in one.

Soon we pulled over in the main square, in front of the most unusual house; ostentatiously painted from top to bottom with biblical scenes. It just seemed completely out of place in that part of the world; more like something you'd expect to see in Mexico.

We hadn't even properly got off the bike before two soldiers armed with machine guns appeared out of thin air. They started questioning us. Their duty was to ensure that we weren't a threat to the village. Once it became obvious that we were just a couple of harmless tourists, they lightened up and invited us to see more of the village. We were then directed through the narrow cobblestone streets to the nearby church, where some kind of celebration was taking place. We were curious to find out more.

The church was just like the ones you see in some European countries; made entirely out of stone, with high walls decorated with colourful stained glass windows. In front of it was yet another group of soldiers guarding the entrance. One informed us that some important priest or bishop type person was visiting the village, and that was why everyone had gathered together. We wanted to join in, but before we were allowed inside, we had to get through yet another security check; this time consisting of two elderly ladies, clearly in charge of the event, maybe even the whole village.

Again, we had to answer some basic questions, like where we'd come from and what we wanted in Alqosh. The final question, probably the most important one, was about our faith. Neither Rebecca nor I wanted to get into a theological debate, so we just confirmed that we were both Christians. Then, and only then, were we allowed inside the church. We were lead by one of the ladies to the front row, where a few local men were shoved over to make space for us.

We didn't understand a thing, yet there was something special about the atmosphere inside. The people around us looked like they were genuinely enjoying themselves. The choir, with all its members dressed in white, was sitting above the congregation, up on the balcony at the back of the church. They were singing in total harmony, probably having rehearsed their performance to perfection. This alone made for a very special atmosphere. But there was something else present there, too.

Being in that little church in Northern Iraq, with heavily armed soldiers outside, made me think of other Christian communities throughout history who have been persecuted or are currently being persecuted, simply because of their faith. It seemed to me that in most cases, ironically, faith thrives in such adverse circumstances and unites people going through hardships. And that's what I felt in Alqosh; a sense of a close-knit community, like in no other church I've ever visited.

After a while I got a bit bored with the church service and decided to go outside. Rebecca stayed put, probably still mesmerised by the whole experience. Once out, one of the soldiers who'd been guarding the main door approached me to chat. Unfortunately, because of the language barrier, we couldn't understand each other. Instead he offered me a cigarette, which I accepted; even though I'm not a smoker, it's something I do sometimes, just to connect with people.

We tried to exchange a few more words, but the conversation was going nowhere. After we'd finished smoking, he smiled and excitedly exclaimed in English "come". There was something he wanted to show me, so I followed.

He rushed off a few steps ahead of me, so briskly that I was barely able to keep up without breaking into a jog. We took one turn after another and soon entered an uninhabited part of the village, far from the church and out of anyone's sight. Even the path turned into overgrowth.

At this point I became pretty worried. I was following a stranger with a machine gun, in a country with a recent history of violence directed at Westerners. We'd entered Iraq proper against our Embassys' advice, and nobody knew where we were. As my mind usually does, I imagined the worse; was I about to be shot or taken hostage...there's a thin line between being adventurous, trusting and just being plain stupid... I was at the soldier's mercy, but it was too late to turn around.

My thoughts continued troubling me until we finally stopped in front of some unimpressive ruins of an old church. It really wasn't anything special, but I was relieved to see this place, to discover that it existed, and that it hadn't all just been a trick to lure me into a secluded area.

The entrance door was locked, so after all this brisk walking (and worrying) we couldn't even get in. The soldier tried to tell me something about it, but I didn't understand him, and I didn't care much at that point.

We soon turned around and went back to the village the same way we'd come. Rebecca was still inside the church, enjoying the atmosphere, unaware of my escapade. As I sat next to her, my heart rate started to slow down.

The whole thing with the soldier brought back to mind a particular situation that had happened more than ten years earlier in India. It was our first travel experience as a couple and our first time in Asia. And it wasn't just any Asian country, it was India; a country known to be particularly challenging for travellers. We didn't expect an easy ride backpacking there.

Worried about our safety, I read every bit of advice I could find. I hung on to every word I read in guide books, as if they were holy books. The more I read, the more paranoid I became. Needless to say, I expected to be robbed and caught out with all the cunning tricks used to rip-off unwitting Western tourists.

One day we went out on a stroll through some remote Himalayan villages. As we were passing one of the houses, an old lady came outside and called us in with a wave of her hand. Curious, we followed. Inside the house she invited us to sit down and brought us two glasses of water. I instantly thought about the cleanliness of the water. Having read the Lonely Planet guidebook from cover to cover, I was obsessed about drinking ONLY bottled water –after thoroughly inspecting the seal to make sure it hadn't been resealed by a local trickster wanting to make a quick buck from unsuspecting travellers.

It's embarrassing to admit now, but I imagined that the water could have been spiked with something and that this seemingly sweet old lady probably wanted to rob us or help someone else rob us. For these two reasons, I was hesitant to take even the tiniest sip. Eventually, not wanting to offend the old lady and battling with my brain to stay rational, I drank it.

The water she gave us was a simple gift to provide us some relief from the heat of the day. That was it. Plain and simple, the lady didn't want anything in return. The gesture came from the kindness of her heart.

It was my first time travelling and I had no experience of the world. My mind was filled with negative stories. Unfortunately, not knowing any different, I took what I read and saw on the TV as truth. Like most people, I'd been conditioned to see the world as a dangerous place. It took me many years to change that view. It was through travelling that I slowly began to understand that, believe it or not, the world is actually a pretty safe place, with the majority of people being kind-hearted and good.

I thought that I'd changed since that time in India, opened up and learned to trust strangers, but in Alqosh I was caught off-guard, I realised that I wasn't quite as open and trusting as I'd thought I was. My thinking was prejudiced, based on fear about Iraq; something that I'd been fed through the ever-present media reporting and images. When my own experience was lacking, my mind grasped for anything, prejudiced or not. Knowledge was the only cure.

St Joseph's

We stayed inside the church until the mass had finished. When exiting, among the slowly moving crowd of people, we stumbled upon a teenage boy named Fadi and started chatting. His English was really good. Meeting him gave us a chance to learn something about the village. Not only was he happy to answer all our questions, he also offered to show us around the village, which we immediately accepted.

I laughed out loud when I realised the first place he chose to take us was the exact same ruined church that the soldier had shown me. The door was still locked, but Fadi knew where to get the key from and this time we managed to get in. He proudly explained that this little church was built more than a thousand years earlier. We later learned that Assyrians, who'd lived in this part of the world for millennia, began to convert from the Mesopotamian religion to Christianity as early as the first century AD. It's funny how just hearing a little of the history of what at first seemed like an unimpressive pile of rubble, transformed it into something pretty awe inspiring.

We continued walking through the village until our tour was interrupted by heavy rainfall. To avoid us all getting drenched, we stopped at the orphanage for girls. One of the nuns invited the three of us inside for a warming cup of tea and chat. It was a nice break and we were grateful for the shelter, but we didn't want to intrude and once it had stopped raining, we thanked her for hospitality and left. As we were leaving I realised that most of our biking clothes and helmets were still sitting on the motorcycle, uncovered, outside the house with the colourful murals. I was expecting everything to be soaked, but when we got to the bike we saw that someone had kindly covered all our gear with a large piece of plastic sheeting to protect it from the rain. They'd also thoughtfully placed a large piece of metal on top to keep the plastic shelter in place.

At that point we considered leaving Alqosh. It was long past our two-hour allotted deadline. We knew that within the next couple of hours we'd need to find a suitable spot for camping while there was still a bit of daylight.

Fadi, wanting to help us, pulled out his mobile phone and called his older cousin, who showed up in his car moments later. The cousin told us that he knew just the right place for us. We jumped on our motorcycle and followed them through the village. On the way to "the place" we stopped over at their home, probably to consult the elders about our situation. Although we didn't know their exact plans for us, we trusted that it would all work out well.

As the two boys were chatting with their family, we looked around. Opposite the house was an old cemetery which instantly drew our attention. Whenever we travel, cemeteries are one of our favourite places to visit. This might sound peculiar, but we find it interesting to see how they differ from country to country. Despite cultural differences, though, there is something about cemeteries that feels utterly universal. As we weren't making a move just yet, Rebecca and I wandered off to explore the graves. The cemetery was entirely Christian, with many large crosses carved in stone. We couldn't understand any of the inscriptions: later we found out that Alqosh is one of few places where people still use Aramaic language; the language of Jesus and John the Baptist, and the root of the Hebrew, Syriac and Arabic alphabets. Aramaic, once widespread throughout the world, is today largely restricted to Northern Iraq, some small parts of Syria, Iran and Turkey.

Though the stroll was enjoyable, we were becoming worried about time. It would soon be getting dark and finding a camping spot when you can't see what's around isn't a pleasant experience. Fadi soon showed up. He confirmed that we'd be spending the night at a nearby monastery.

Once again we followed and soon arrived at the gates of a large monastery complex. Before leaving, the boys talked to the security guard at the gate and he agreed to let us through. The sun had now set and we had nowhere else to go. For better or worse, this was our place for the night.

First though, we needed to find a person in charge, somebody who could tell us where to camp. We began our search, but surprisingly there was nobody in sight. The only person we could find was the guard at the main gate, who couldn't say a word in English and was glued to his post.

After walking around the monastery for a while we finally got chatting to a monk taking an evening stroll. Strangely enough, he was from the Czech Republic. Even though he spoke no English, we could just about understand each other thanks to some similarities between the Polish and Czech languages. He suggested we head towards the adjacent St Joseph's Children's Home, where he was certain we could stay overnight.

We entered the grounds of the children's home and found it equally quiet. After a short while a young priest showed up and invited us in for a cup of tea and some sweets. He was friendly and chatty, though it seemed he wasn't in a position to decide what to do with us. Once we'd finished our drinks, he invited the boys in to meet us. Baring more sweet treats, they all came to check out their curious foreign guests.

Having been on the road for about a year, we'd got used being treated like some kind of visiting entertainment. It didn't bother us; in fact it was equally amusing for us.

Most of the older boys spoke good English and the younger ones knew at least some basic phrases. Though slightly shy at the beginning, it didn't take long for them to warm to us and very soon they started to bombard us with questions. Filled with curiosity and excitement, they were talking over each other, trying their best to grab our attention.

One of the boys brought more tea and even more sweets. Seeing that I enjoyed them, he disappeared again and this time brought a whole carrier bag full for me. All this generosity felt like it was way too much, but they wouldn't take "no" for an answer. The priest was in agreement. I tried to share them with everyone, but to my surprise, none of the kids wanted any. They just weren't interested.

After some chatter and plenty of jokes, especially from the older boys, the priest announced that it was time for dinner. Almost in the blink of an eye the boys disappeared and we were left alone with the priest again. He offered us a place to sleep inside the house, but not wanting to overstay the welcome, we suggested camping in the grounds. Hesitantly, he agreed and took us outside to find a nice flat spot. He then went inside and left us to unpack our camping gear. Almost just as quickly as they'd disappeared the boys reappeared bringing two large trays of food and drinks with them. It was a welcomed gift. We didn't fancy cooking, and stuffing our faces with the bag of sweets wouldn't have been a good idea. They left us in peace to finish our meal but soon returned to take the trays back; most of them wanted to spend more time with us. They were buzzing with excitement. We decided that the best way to engage the group was to find them something to do. Helping us pitch the tent was the obvious choice. They loved the idea.

Each of them wanted to be involved in the process; to see everything, to touch everything, and to know everything. They had hundreds of questions, literally. This simple task, which would normally take us just a few minutes, stretched to hours of evening fun.

Eventually the priest came out to call them all back inside, probably thinking that we were being pestered. We really weren't, though. But it was getting late and they needed to wake up early the next morning for school. Reluctantly, yet very obediently, they wished us a good night and went back inside.

Our first day in Iraq was over. It had been full of surprises, we couldn't have hoped for a better turn of events. We'd heard a lot of good things about Kurdish people, but that day we got to experience real Assyrian and Iraqi hospitality.

By the time we woke up the next day, the boys were already in school. The sun was getting stronger by the minute and as there was nobody around, we began packing up; the idea of leaving so soon without saying goodbye didn't seem right, but waiting the whole day with nothing to do wasn't appealing either.

We were ready to leave when a car stopped just outside the main door. It was the driver for the Children's Home, whom we'd met briefly the previous night. He'd just returned from dropping the kids off at school. He came to say "Hello" and to invite us for breakfast. It was good we'd accepted the invite because when we got there the food was already prepared and waiting for us.

As we were munching away, the driver offered to take us up to the ancient monastery complex above the village. We accepted, seeing it as a good way to kill some time while waiting for the boys to come back from school. We set off after we'd finished our breakfast. After a short drive we arrived at the bottom of a mountain. Far up at the very top was our destination. It was an ancient monastery, which gave the impression of a fortress, built high up into the rock face in this remote corner of the world. Excited to see it up close, we began climbing.

The place was indeed a hidden treasure. The Rabban Hormizd Monastery, as it's called, was founded around 640 AD and throughout the centuries it gained extreme importance. Even though it was built upon an enormous rock, it's said that the monastery was too exposed to attacks to remain functioning. In the 19th century, with financial assistance from the Vatican, a new monastery was built in a safer location about a mile away. The monks relocated there and Rabban Hormizd became a distant memory.

When we finally got up there, the main part of the monastery was closed off, but we could still wander around and see where the monks used to live. Their cells were also carved out of solid rock. There were neither doors nor any other kind of protection from the harshness of the elements, and it's likely they had no such luxuries as fires to keep them warm either.

Unfortunately, the monastery was very run down and slowly becoming a ruin. Time and the elements seemed to have been merciless to it.

When the sightseeing was over, we returned back to St. Joseph's. The driver dropped us off and continued on his way to the school. He soon returned with a bunch of very excited boys, clearly happy to see us again. This time it was the motorcycle that became the main point of interest. Every lad wanted to sit on it and have his picture taken. I offered to take each of them for a short ride, which made for a pretty special memory for us all. They were teeming with excitement. It took me almost an hour to make sure everyone had his turn.

Soon they had to leave for food, and though we would have loved to have stayed longer, it was time to hit the road.

We stayed in touch with one of the boys. About a year after our visit to Alqosh, he emailed us with some bad news. Because of the threat from ISIS, the whole Children's Home had to be evacuated. Inevitably the boys were separated; some even had to leave the country.

The Peacock Angel

Although we worried about returning to the Iraqi military checkpoint, going through was a breeze. The soldiers didn't even bother to stop us. Their job was to protect the city and as we were leaving, I guess we were no longer seen as a threat.

We made our way to a town called Lalish, located just 30 miles from Alqosh. Again, we didn't know what to expect, and again we were greeted by heavily armed soldiers. But on this occasion, instead of giving us a hard time, they gave us a very warm welcome. We chatted for a while and took some pictures together. Before letting us go, they asked us to take our boots off. As strange as it sounded, we were told that Lalish could only be entered barefoot.

We left the motorcycle, our boots and socks with the soldiers and walked on to see what this place was all about. We soon realised that Lalish was completely unique. Its architecture, customs and the ever-present colourful peacock, which was painted on walls and doors, were all something that we'd never seen anywhere before.

We didn't know it at the time, but Lalish holds the holiest temple in the Yazidi religion which by the way is one of the oldest religions on Earth. Lalish is the spiritual heartland of the Yazidi people, and is like the Vatican is to Catholics, I suppose. But unlike the Vatican, Lalish is tiny. Despite its small size, the site was packed with an eclectic mix of interesting buildings, ranging from small huts to larger domes.

It was fairly quiet when we got there; with only one small group of visitors (most likely Iraqi) and a handful of locals wandering around. Not knowing where to go or what to expect, we followed the other visitors and soon entered an underground tomb.

Past the main entrance, there was a dark pool of water to our right. This water is known as the Lake of Azreal; Azreal being the Angel of Death. Some Yazidis believe that he washes his sword in this pool after taking a soul. Others claim that this is where Azreal brings the souls of the dead to be judged. Luckily he didn't show himself during our visit.

Further on, through a small door, we walked into a large hall; it was spacious but dim and cold. There were no windows and only a handful of lights. The floor surface was smooth, having been polished by the feet of visitors who'd been there over the centuries. The place was steeped in history, stories, experiences; we could sense it in the air.

The pillars supporting the whole structure were decorated colourfully, wrapped in copious layers of sheets of silk, brought and left there by devout pilgrims. Innumerable knots were tied on every single sheet, screwing the fabric to its maximum capacity. It is said that Yazidis do it to solve their troubles.

From there we walked through another small door and came to the second room, filled with rows of big old dirty clay pots, hundreds of them. We were told that these ancient pots hold oil used in religious ceremonies and rituals that are held in Lalish Temple throughout the year.

As we walked further, we came across a small group of visitors, possibly a family, who had gathered by one of the walls. They were trying their best to throw a small piece of cloth towards the wall, carefully aiming to get it to stay up on a ledge. It was a "wishing rock". Those who succeeded would have their wishes granted. It was no surprise that everyone was eager to try. It looked like fun, yet there was a level of seriousness attached to it, too. Of course there was; who wouldn't want their wishes to be granted? The more we walked around and saw, the more our minds boggled with curiosity and a desire to know more about this peculiar religion and its followers.

Next we entered the tomb. There was nothing else in the room except a large sarcophagus completely covered in a black shroud. Not knowing the importance of this place, we soon left. Little did we know, Sheikh Adi ibn Musafir who rests there, was the founder of the Yazidi religion; he's believed to be an incarnation of Melek Taus, a benevolent peacock angel who according to the Yazidi faith is the true creator and ruler of the universe. I learned later that circling the tomb eight times was another way to have your wishes granted. We missed our chance.

We left Lalish pretty perplexed. Only one day earlier we'd entered Iraq believing that Islam would be the only religion we'd encounter, but we'd already found ourselves travelling from one religious minority to another. It was a completely different Iraq to what we'd expected to experience.

Sadly, towards the end of 2014, only months after we left Northern Iraq, many Yazidi cities were attacked by ISIS fighters. The violence was labelled by the perpetrators as a "forced conversion campaign", but it was much more than that. For centuries Yazidi people had been persecuted by jihadist sects who perceived Melek Taus, the peacock angel, as Satan. For them, Yazidis are devil worshippers.

As a result of this violent campaign it was reported that around 5000 Yazidi men were murdered, and at least 7000 women were kidnapped and sold into sexual slavery. Many others fled to the mountains to save themselves from brutal attacks. ISIS' action against the Yazidi population resulted in approximately half a million refugees. Thousands sought refuge in Lalish. Although the holy city remained under Yazidi control, it was and still is under grave threat from ISIS.

Creatures of the night

From Lalish we drove towards the capital of Iraqi Kurdistan, Erbil. But instead of going there directly, we chose the long way which took us through the villages and mountains of Northern Kurdistan.

We cruised slowly from one military checkpoint to another, and the further north we went, the fewer checkpoints we encountered. Soon we entered the mountains. We then continued driving from one village to another until the sun started setting.

Finding a camping spot was rather easy; the place was close to the main road, but hidden enough so that nobody could see us. It seemed like a peaceful spot. And as a bonus, right in front of us was a beautiful view of the valley.

After pitching our tent, we made ourselves supper. We then sat on the grass in front of our tent to eat our food and enjoy the orange sun slowly disappearing behind the hills. Suddenly, far in the distance, I heard some loud and unfamiliar noises. It sounded like a mix between a dog howling and a baby screaming, but it was neither. It was definitely an animal, or rather a pack of animals spread throughout the valley. They were communicating, perhaps even hunting together.

The sound didn't worry me too much because it was coming from the other side of the valley, far away from us. Whatever it was, it soon quietened and after a while we'd forgotten all about it.

By the time we'd finished eating, the sun had set completely. We brushed our teeth and climbed in our tent to sleep.

In the middle of the night, we were woken up by the same sound, but this time it seemed to be coming from around our tent. As previously, the noise was spread over a wide territory and we were now in the middle of it. I imagined there were probably at least a dozen creatures surrounding us. I was frightened. The only animal I could think of as producing such a sound was either a wild dog or a hyena. Being zipped up in a small tent without any means of protecting ourselves and unable to see what was happening outside, I felt vulnerable. There wasn't that much I could do, but without thinking, I picked up my motorcycle boots and started banging them against each other, in the hope that the noise would scare the creatures off. Luckily, it did the trick; the mysterious unwelcomed visitors disappeared back into the darkness of the night.

To this day I don't know what animal they were. Having previously misjudged the sounds of nature (mistaking deer for bears), I know better than to jump to any conclusions. I tried asking locals, but nobody was able to give me a definite answer. I will never be certain, but based on research I believe it was a cackle (pack) of striped hyenas. Although the population of these nocturnal animals is rapidly declining, they are still common in these parts of the world.

The hyena is primarily a scavenger, but attacks on humans have occurred on very rare occasions, though I don't believe we were in any real danger that night. They were probably as surprised to find us there as we were to hear them. Despite the fright, I believe it was a gift to encounter those rare animals in their natural habitat.

Kindness without limits

We woke up to a beautiful morning. With the sun still low, we hit the road as soon as we'd packed the tent away. As like every other day in Iraqi Kurdistan, we didn't have an exact plan, the only plan was to keep our eyes peeled for something different, something worth stopping for. So when we drove past a signpost indicating a tourist attraction, a very rare occurrence on this road, there was no way we could ignore it. That's how we found the Shanidar cave.

We parked the motorcycle at the bottom of the mountain and started ascending towards the cave, a fair walk from the parking lot. It was already around midday and the sun was merciless; Rebecca, being sensitive to the sun, soon decided to stay behind and wait in the shade. I continued on my own, not far along the route I was joined by two other visitors, both guys. They were going to the same place, so it was only natural to walk together. One spoke English. His name was Taha and I soon learned that he was a Kurdish politician from Erbil; the other was Jafar, his guest, visiting from Iran. They were both pleasant company.

Because of the heat it was a strenuous climb, but the view compensated for it. In fact, the walk itself proved more rewarding than the cave, which was just a large hollowing in the rock. Apparently it's a place with great archaeological significance, but without the background information it was nothing special.

On our way down Taha suggested spending the rest of the day together. There were some other interesting places in the area he wanted to show us. He seemed friendly and trustworthy, but before agreeing I needed to see if Rebecca was OK with the plan.

Once the sightseeing was over, I joined her in the shade. Taha came over, too. He introduced himself and renewed his invitation, this time to both of us. There was something very kind and warm about him, which helped when making our decision.

When travelling, we're usually pretty careful about whom we trust; a healthy amount of openness with a dose of caution goes a long way. Over the years we've learned to rely on our gut feeling which has so far kept us safe (touch wood).

We agreed to follow Taha and his friend. Before heading off, he suggested we make a stop in a nearby restaurant, apparently one of his favourites, for a taste of Kurdish cuisine. We liked the sound of that.

He drove slowly to make it easier for us to tail him. It was easy to keep up at first, until we entered the city and the traffic got denser. At one of the many intersections we got separated. To make matters worse, without exaggeration, pretty much every vehicle on the road was just like Taha's - a white Toyota pickup. I'd never seen so many white Toyotas. And the number plates were of no use whatsoever because they were all in Arabic. There was nothing distinguishing his Toyota pickup from the umpteen others surrounding us. Luckily we found each other eventually, and after that we followed his car like we were its shadow.

When we arrived at our first stop, he pulled over, and excited about the prospect of trying some local food, we quickly jumped off the bike and followed him into the restaurant. We couldn't wait to order... until we realised that the favourite eatery was a Kebab shop. We've never been fans of kebab, and it really wasn't what we'd expected. With hidden disappointment, we allowed Taha to order for us. We tried what we were served, and, to our surprise it was without doubt the best kebab we'd ever tasted. It was made with good quality meat and plenty of seasoning. It came with a selection of salads, freshly baked bread and other tasty side dishes.

The restaurant was buzzing with locals, all enjoying their afternoon meal. Rebecca was the only woman there. Despite that, she didn't notice anyone staring at her or being unwelcoming, quite the opposite, everyone seemed friendly and respectful.

When we were close to finishing our food, Taha took the initiative and before we'd even realised he'd paid for everyone. We weren't just his company, we were his guests, and were treated with the same amount of kindness and hospitality as his friend from Iran.

When leaving we were told that we were heading to a city not too far away, a place selling the best ice-cream in Kurdistan. This time we knew to trust his judgement. Besides, we were all heading in the same direction, Erbil, so following somebody who knew the area made perfect sense.

We took a scenic route through the Zagros Mountains, which are the largest in the region. The view was far-reaching and breathtaking. Taha was proud of his country and wanted us to experience its beauty for ourselves.

About an hour later we arrived in a small atmospheric city. We parked in the centre, just off the main road. As was our habit, we took out our chains and began locking our gear. Having noticed what we were doing, Taha came over and with confidence in his voice said: "There's no Ali Baba here, your things won't disappear. This is Kurdistan." He was right; though busy, it was a close-knit community and no one stole our gear. When we came back everything was just as we'd left it.

The ice-cream was as advertised, delicious. Thanks to Taha's choice we ended up with a massive portion that we could barely finish. Afterwards, without saying a word, he once again paid for us all; again not giving us a chance to oppose his decision. After all, he was a strong-willed politician, who'd once been a freedom fighter against Saddam's regime, and if he wanted to pay, he was paying. We don't like to take advantage of people's kindness, but the last thing we'd want to do is offend someone. Sometimes you just have to learn to take as well as give. So we thanked him, once again, for his generosity.

Before getting back to our vehicles, our new friend called his wife to let her know that there would be two more guests for dinner that evening.

On our way to the house I stopped at the petrol station to fill up. When I went to pay, I was shocked to find that he'd pulled over behind the station and got to the till before me. For me, such hospitality was unheard of & we were receiving so much of it that it was becoming almost too much to accept.

We got to Taha's home about half an hour later. The house was large and modern, located in a nice neighbourhood; a place worthy of a respected politician. Inside he introduced us to his family; his wife, children and cousins. Soon after arriving we were shown to our bedroom and assumed we'd be spending the night. By the time we'd changed our clothes and cleaned up from the road, the dinner was ready. There were about twelve of us sitting around the table, and there was enough food for at least double the number. It was a proper Kurdish home-cooked feast, with lots of welcoming faces & merriment.

During and after dinner, our host engaged us with numerous stories from the time when he was a young boy and was fighting for Kurdish autonomy. He told us about having to leave his home in 1975 to escape Saddam Husain's attacks on Kurdish people, about his father's passing away whilst in exile, and about the many years he'd spent in the mountains fighting for his country. Kurdish fighters are called Peshmergas which literally means "the ones who face death". Though he was no longer a soldier, Taha continued to serve his country; as a politician.

We still keep in touch with his family from time to time; about a year after we'd met he sent us a beautiful photo-book of Kurdistan, filled with snaps a French journalist friend had managed to take during some difficult times in Iraqi Kurdistan when it was closed to foreign journalists.

Being around this man made me think about Kurds: I found it perplexing but also inspiring that people who have been oppressed for so long and have suffered so greatly, are able to possess so much kindness and openness towards strangers.

Lost in translation

We left Eribl in good moods. It was only our third day in Kurdistan but we already knew that this country was going to become one of our favourites.

Our next destination, Sulaymaniyah, was around 150 miles away, close enough for a day's travel. Again, there were two roads to choose from; one passing through the mountains, the other one near the enemy lines. The choice was a no-brainer.

Around half way to Suli (as locals call Sulaymaniyah) we stopped by the side of the road to make something to eat. It was a pleasant spot for cooking; shaded with a little water pool on the side. I fired up the cooker; first made some tea and shortly afterwards we got a few veggies frying.

We wondered who we'd meet this time. We knew from experience that sooner or later our strange activity would attract someone's attention. It pretty much always did. The food was still cooking when the first visitor showed up; a guy, maybe in his forties, wearing traditional Kurdish clothing, still very popular daywear throughout the country. It looks almost like a uniform, usually all brown, black or khaki, and consists of two main parts. The first part, a rank, is worn like trousers, but is usually twice as wide. The second part, a chogha, is like a jacket; the bottom of it is tucked inside the rank. A large scarf is wrapped around the waist like a wide belt.

We invited him to join us. There was still some tea left so we shared it with him. Our new companion didn't speak much English, though he tried his best to use every word he knew, "water", "sky", "hand", which was fun but didn't really help us understand each other. With a little body language and gesturing thrown into the mix, we soon learned that his name was Abbas. He stayed with us till the meal was ready.

Rebecca divided the food equally between the three of us and we all tucked in, he rather reluctantly at first. It was a simple but flavoursome dish. Our guest was curious about the spices we used and examined them carefully. Most were foreign to him, but the ones he knew, he happily named in Kurdish.

After the meal was over, we washed the dishes, packed our gear and were about to leave when Abbas in his extremely limited English said "You, my home". It seemed obvious what he wanted. We looked at each other, smiled and instantly knew the answer - it had to be "yes". We quickly got ready to follow him, but instead of getting back into his car to lead the way he shook our hands and said "Good Bye". Confused, we wished him farewell and left just after him.

We continued towards Suli as before, occasionally stopping to take pictures. We didn't expect to ever see Abbas again, yet there he was, more than half an hour later, standing by the side of the road, looking like he was waiting for somebody. He smiled at us and said "You, my home?" as if wanting to confirm that we were still coming. He'd waited for us. We agreed once again, but this time we followed his car. When we arrived, the family came out on to the street to meet and greet us. Abbas and his wife had six children; three daughters and three sons. The eldest daughter brought water to share. We then slowly made our way inside the house, which was basic, but cosy and very well taken care of. Apart from a TV unit in the corner, carpet on the floor and a clock ticking away on the wall, there was no furniture, no tables or chairs, so we all sat on the floor in the middle of what seemed to be the main room.

They were a lovely family, so warm and joyful. The daughters studied English at school and had some rudimentary vocabulary. They pulled out their school books to show Rebecca and I their homework.

They were happy to have us there, but we didn't want to intrude so after a couple of hours we announced that we were going to leave to continue our journey. Without hesitation the family invited us to stay overnight; using Google translator to help them express what they wanted to say. It seemed to work pretty well. They didn't want us to leave and Rebecca and I were having a good time, so we accepted their invitation and looked forward to learning a bit more about the family.

Later in the afternoon we all moved into the kitchen, where we sat on the floor in a small circle. The food was placed in the middle. We could see that despite not having much, they brought all they could to make us feel welcome; they gave us the best offerings, too.

After the meal more family members arrived to take a look at us. We quickly became the main attraction in the village. They phoned a cousin who'd spent time living in the UK, to act as a translator. He used to live in London and spoke English fluently. Having someone to translate was way better than using Google, but it also meant that the number of questions increased substantially. They wanted to know everything about us.

One question proved particularly controversial; it was about our religious views. In our travel experience this has been the most frequently asked question, the second is how many children we have. Anyway, in answer to the one regarding our religious background, Rebecca tended to reply that we were both Christians, just for simplicity really because people had been very perplexed and concerned when we'd previously tried to explain that we weren't religious people.

In fact we were both baptised and brought up Catholic, but as we've grown up and learnt more about life and the world, we moved away from our upbringing and now don't consider ourselves religious. At some point in our journey I became tired of listening to my wife telling others her little white lie. So before arriving in Kurdistan Rebecca and I chatted about her telling people that we were both Christians, and we decided that I would speak for myself in future. So having all that in mind and feeling pretty relaxed with Abbas and his family, I answered "I don't believe in God". Nobody was expecting that, they were completely dumbstruck. You could have heard a pin drop!

The silence which engulfed the room seemed to last an eternity. I couldn't believe myself and my big fat mouth; out of all the places in the world where I could have 'come out', I chose Iraqi Kurdistan. Rebecca quickly came to the rescue and explained that what I'd meant to say was that we ARE both Christians but don't practice regularly. They accepted that with sighs of relief and ecstatic nods.

The clock struck ten and it was time to prepare ourselves for sleep. We were given blankets and two thin mattresses, and were shown that we'd be sleeping in the living room. Just before hitting the sack, we left the room to go to the toilet and to brush our teeth. It was located outside, so we had to leave the house. As we opened the front door, we couldn't believe our eyes. The whole family was getting ready to sleep... outside, on the terrace!

We tried explaining that we'd sleep outside, happily. It was clear they weren't going to accept that suggestion so we tried to explain, mostly using body language and gestures, that there was enough space in the living room for all of us. But we were guests and the family wanted us to feel comfortable. Our comfort was the priority for them. We were given the only sleeping room and the family ended up on a concrete floor outdoors. Again we'd never in our lives experienced hospitality like it. It gave our understanding of kindness a completely new dimension.

The next day we woke up early, tidied the room and opened the doors. We found Abbas, his wife and one of the youngest children asleep on the kitchen floor. They must have moved there in the middle of the night; we assumed because it had been cold outside. They were uncomfortable, yet still, they didn't want to disturb us by entering the room.

After sitting down to share breakfast with everyone, we packed up and got the bike ready. The whole family came out on the street to give us hugs and wish us a happy journey. We posed for a few final pictures, thanked them from our hearts and left, quite reluctantly.

Before coming to Kurdistan, we'd heard about the exceptional hospitality of Kurds in the region, but to experience it first hand was really something else.

The oppressed

Our next stay was with Henrik; Rebecca had found his profile on Couch Surfing and having decided that he'd be an interesting person to spend a first nights with, she sent him a guest request. He was a Swedish headmaster living and working in Sulaymaniyah as the head of a local school. He'd been living in the country for more than a year.

Our first challenge was to find the right address. It had been a while since our sat-nav packed up on us and not having a map, we just had to keep asking for directions. Thankfully, Henrik's flat was located close to the centre, on one of the main streets, so everyone knew where to send us.

Our host proved to be a friendly giant; close to 7 foot tall, he was a grey haired Swede with an open mind and a huge dollop of humour to add to every occasion. We hit it off right away. The first evening he took us to a restaurant to meet some of his circle of friends, which consisted largely of expats and local social workers. It was a fun evening, filled with interesting conversations. Everyone was happy to share their stories about Kurdistan with us. We also got some useful tips about places to visit, both within the city and around the country.

As recommended, the next day we headed straight to the Amna Suraka Museum, the museum of war crimes in Kurdistan, otherwise known as the Red Prison. In this prison-turned-museum thousands of Kurds were tortured and executed until it was liberated in 1991. Now the museum is a vivid reminder of the terror and oppression that still stains Kurdistan.

The next day we left the city to further explore the country. We headed east. There were a few places we wanted to visit. One of them was Halabja, the place where, in 1988, a massacre against the Kurdish people took place. It's estimated that up to 5,000 people were murdered in a chemical attack. It still remains the largest chemical attack in history directed at civilians in a populated area.

It was less than 50 miles from Suli to Halabja. The autonomous Kurdistan is rather small; any biker could easily drive across the whole region in less than a day.

We headed straight for the memorial site which also held a recently built museum. When we got there, it looked like the place was abandoned. The only "people" we could see were stony twisted life-size human statues. They were the sculptures created in memory of the genocide victims. Amongst them was an old rusty pick-up truck; an actual vehicle which was used to move corpses in the aftermath of the attack. Without anybody around, it was an eerie site.

Inside we met a guy working for the museum. He was happy to show us around. We soon found out that he was actually one of few survivors. He willingly became our guide, directing us through the exhibition and answering all our questions. In the first room there were more life-size human sculptures, made to look as realistic as possible, all twisted in agony, dying or already dead from the poisonous gas. The second room was filled with thousands of pictures, taken shortly after the unthinkable event. Looking at all those images of helpless villagers, many of whom were women and children, murdered in the masses for simply having being born Kurdish, made us feel physically sick. We were told that to trick the victims and kill more people, the gas was given a sweetly pleasant smell.

After the chemical attack in Halabja, thousands of Kurds escaped; either to the mountains or across the border to Iran. I couldn't even begin to comprehend the pain that those people went through.

Visiting Halabja was overwhelming, but it was necessary. Hearing about the chemical attack on the news allowed a certain detachment, but being in the actual town where it took place, seeing those images and the scenes recreated, changes one's perception. It was painful, just as it should have been and what we saw there will remain with us.

On our way back to the city we accidentally on purpose got lost; we had plenty of time and wanted to explore. We found an ambient little village. Wandering off-track paid off.

Just off the main street there was a sweet shop, full of people. We went inside and ordered tea and baklava; a sickly sweet dessert pastry made with chopped nuts, sweetened and held together with syrup or honey. The baklava was tasty, but watching locals slowly sipping their tea and passing time was even more rewarding. The space was filled with laughter, comradery and ever-present cigarette smoke. Men of all ages played backgammon, some for fun, others competitively. The atmosphere was light and cheerful.

After two rounds of tea we were ready to go, so I went to the main counter to settle the bill. The owner bearing a big smile on his face meaningfully placed his hand on his heart area, to show us that there was no need to pay. It was yet another gesture of kindness added to our ever-growing list.

The Autonomous Kurdish Republic was really special; pretty much everywhere we stopped we met someone offering us something. It could be anything ranging from inviting us to their home, offering us free food or a drink, a friendly chat, or simply smiling with warmth.

Kindness towards strangers takes little effort and costs close to nothing, yet it makes a massive impact on visitors like us.

I wondered why such kindness seems to be so rare in many places these days, especially back where we're from. Most of us seem to close ourselves to strangers, as if the old saying "stranger - danger" were true. Ironically, out of all the nations that we've encountered during our travels, it was the endlessly oppressed Kurds that were the most kind and open towards outsiders. Although, I have to say that we've received some kindness and warmth in every single country we've visited.

The refugee crisis

Before leaving Kurdistan we were offered the chance to visit a refugee camp. It was the beginning of 2014; even though the civil war in Syria had started 3 years earlier, the refugee crisis wasn't yet on the front of every European newspaper.

The camp we were to visit was just outside Suli, in a small place called Arbat. It was reported to have around 6000 people living there at the time. As we drove up to the gates, our view was obscured by plumes of dust. Once it had settled, we saw hundreds of white UNICEF tents spread across the plain. The entire site was surrounded with wire fencing.

Inside we were greeted warmly by Karzan and Awara, who'd both been working there since it opened as a transit camp eight months earlier. Having both previously been Kurdish refugees in Iran, they were acutely aware of the difficulties faced by Kurdish Syrians who were arriving there. Awara told us that his name meant 'refugee': a name aptly given to him by his parents because of the circumstances in which he came into the world – it would remain a constant reminder of all that his family had gone through before arriving back in Iraqi Kurdistan some years later.

One of the tents near the entrance was busy with the commotion of people; hygiene products and other necessities were being distributed to the residents. Mothers stood or sat waiting in line for their turn, chatting, while their children played around them.

The camp had two bakeries and a small shop selling everything from groceries to toys. Next to the shop was a tent designated as a medical centre, and another as a school. We entered the school tent. There, in the first class we saw the pupils had some kind of examination and were sitting at desks, facing the whiteboard, heads down working studiously.

The headmaster was kind enough to talk to us. He explained that most children had 4 hours of schooling a day, but the lack of sufficient course books and the dirty dusty building made conditions difficult for both teachers and pupils. When it came to teaching materials they simply had to make the best of whatever was sent to them.

The school was housed in a number of tents, which had been put up inside an unfinished building that was once used for cattle. During high temperatures a strong stench of manure spread throughout the classrooms. In spite of the difficulties, the staff had made the space colourful and inviting, and the children we saw were all engaged and even seemed to be enjoying their lessons.

Later we made our way past the playground, where it was nice to see children just being children; running, jumping, smiling, and laughing. Just across the way, we saw some teenage boys shooting pool in a small shack. They invited me to have a game and, much to their amusement, I potted the white with my first shot.

One of the refugees employed at the camp, invited us to his family's tent. Inside, his mother greeted us with a big smile and a cup of sweet tea. The main living space was simple, yet carpeted, with thin sleeping mattresses & a few cushions. There were two small bird cages hanging above us, with a pretty little bird in each. Despite the difficult conditions and small number of personal possessions, it had been made homely and was spotlessly clean.

A little while later one of her daughters, Shinda, joined us. She told us that she used to have a job, but after two months the position was given to someone else to rotate limited work opportunities. We were hit by the sense of boredom that this bright young woman must have felt having nothing to do all day, and nowhere to go either. Back in Syria she had been studying at university, with just one year left to do before her graduation. We were told that many men had jobs outside the camp, while the majority of women spent their days around the tents looking after their offspring.

This small refugee camp was just the tip of the iceberg. Hundreds of thousands of people had been forced to flee Syria. These people were Kurds too, the same people who'd showed us hospitality throughout Iraqi Kurdistan, invited us into their homes, fed us and generally looked after us... Being there in the midst of the growing crisis allowed us to see refugees not just as statistical numbers or news stories, but as real people.

Less than two years after our visit, Shinda, her brother and mother finally made their way to Europe. Not seeing a chance of returning back to Syria, she's now settling in Germany.

You could say that she's one of the fortunate ones; one of those who not only had the means to flee, but also survived the journey.

Real nomads

After leaving Iraq, we went on exploring Eastern Turkey, the most remote corner of the country, covered with green hills and large uninhabited spaces. Occasionally we'd come across small nomadic communities living in tents to look after their animals. At one point, spontaneously, we stopped by one family.

The nomads were out in the field, herding their sheep. They were simple-living people, sleeping in large tents most of the year, raising their animals. We parked the bike and walked towards them to say hello. The group consisted of around ten to fifteen people of all ages, men, women and children. Despite the language barrier, they understood that we wanted to help and accepted our presence.

I started chasing the sheep, copying what the nomads were doing. The objective was simple, to find a lamb and make it go from one end of the field to the other. Surprisingly, though sounding simple enough, the task wasn't easy. I threw myself into it, running this way and that with the other guys. Rebecca spent her time playing with the children, who'd taken a real shine to her, and later she climbed to the top of a hill with the women to collect water for the night. By becoming useful, we quickly became a part of the group.

After the herding was done, we got invited by one of the families to their tent. It was an honour. As expected, the inside was very basic, a lot more basic than the tent we'd visited in the refugee camp a couple of days previously, here there were also a few thin mattresses, some pillows and blankets, and a make-shift kitchen just outside the front door, but there wasn't anything homely about this tent. We sat on the floor with the rest of the family, one daughter and a son. Soon after we'd sat, the daughter brought bread, homemade cheese and sugary tea for us all to share. During our travels we've learnt to gracefully accept all such offerings.

We felt so good there that we decided to camp with them overnight. The family offered us space on their tent floor, but not wanting to intrude, especially with memories of Abbas and his family sleeping on the porch outside to give us their sleeping space, we opted to pitch our own tent.

I brought our camping gear and we started setting up. The nomads gathered around to watch us. The young boy we'd just shared food and tea with came to help. Visibly not at all satisfied with how our tent looked, off he went with the look of someone trying to fix a serious problem.

Soon enough there he was with a handful of sturdy twigs in his hand, and around the tent he went, securing it with these additional pegs. He beamed at the final result and his effort paid off with claps from his audience. With a gleam in his eye the boy's father then sent him away to fetch something. He hurried off and soon returned with a double mattress; before rushing off again. The second time he brought pillows and a large blanket. The pride in his face was a real picture; there was barely enough space but he managed to fit everything in. The family wanted to ensure we'd be comfortable. Indeed, that night we slept like logs on our soft bed. It would have been pointless to refuse, mainly because these people who were showing us so much acceptance, would have most likely been offended. For those of us who are naturally givers, learning to also take with gratitude is a valuable lesson gained from travelling.

We woke up early, as the sun was starting to peek through the horizon. Our nomad friends were already awake and busying themselves with various tasks. In this hot climate, early morning or late afternoon is the best time to do chores.

The family we'd sat with the night before invited us for breakfast, but this time we declined; they clearly had little to share and we didn't want to take anything more from them. We had two beautiful boxes of sweets we'd been given by a generous sweet shop owner in Kurdistan to send to our mothers. We decided to give them to the family as a thank you for their hospitality.

Spending a day with them felt like a great privilege, but being able to move on was an even greater one. I used to think that a nomadic lifestyle was synonymous with freedom, until realising that it isn't always the case. Freedom is a choice, not a matter of survival.

The nomads we met were leading a simple and seemingly happy life surrounded by family and nature, but it wasn't the romantic nomadic freedom I'd once envisaged. Again we found ourselves feeling grateful for the freedom we have, true freedom to go wherever we please and to do whatever we want.

Sleeping rough

Our first destination after returning from Iraq was Mardin. It's said to be one of the most beautiful cities in Turkey. It was dark when we arrived. That night was to be our long-awaited stay in a hotel night, so we hadn't minded pushing and doing the extra kilometres to get there. Tired and hungry, we began searching for a room within our budget, which proved to be much harder than we'd anticipated. Mardin is an extremely popular tourist destination and despite having many hotels, they were all either fully booked or way beyond our budget. It soon became clear that there was no chance of finding anything reasonable within the city that night; we'd have to leave and check the outskirts for something cheaper or worst case scenario somewhere to pitch our tent.

We followed the main road out. Despite it being late, cars were whizzing in both directions. We quickly grew desperate to find a place to sleep, any place, camping didn't seem like a viable option. The land was impenetrable; steep and stony with lots of spiky bushes restricting any attempts to venture off the main road.

It was like driving through a desert of nothingness. We were desperate for a rest. After driving pointlessly for about an hour, we'd finally had enough and pulled over at a petrol station. That was it, like it or not, we weren't going anywhere else. We were aching all over, hungry and completely exhausted.

At that time of night the petrol station was dead quiet; ours was the only vehicle there. Sleeping on the floor next to the motorcycle seemed like the only viable option. But before taking out our camping mats, we went inside to introduce ourselves to the staff and seek their approval. Two young guys welcomed us with cups of tea. Once again Google translator proved helpful. We learned that the boys were both Kurdish. They were happy to hear that we'd just returned from Iraqi Kurdistan, and wanted to see some pictures.

Though it was fun to talk to them, our exhaustion soon caught up with us. Rebecca and I needed to get some sleep. But instead of agreeing to let us sleep outside, they suggested that we use one of their back rooms for the night. There was no bed there, but it was clean and much better than the concrete ground outside. They said we could stay there till their shift ended at 6 a.m. We didn't need to be asked twice. But not wanting to get them into any trouble, we made sure to wake up long before their shift was over. After vacating the room, we shared a quick cup of coffee with our hosts, but this time they seemed exhausted and nowhere near as chatty as the night before. We thanked them once again and left.

We'd slept a mere few hours but left the station in good moods, ready to face Mardin once again.

The city looked completely different at daybreak. It was lifeless, serene and inviting; the complete opposite to what we'd seen the night before. Most places were still closed, so we decided to use this time to stroll around the town.

The old part of the city was without a doubt spectacular; it had this touristy yet unobtrusive Turkish charm about it. Mixing commerce and history together is something that Turks seem to have mastered to perfection, at least in some places.

At some point we ventured far off the main streets and found ourselves in a more rural part of the city; a modest part where old houses were slowly crumbling, and a few scrawny chickens were scavenging the streets for something to eat. The profits from tourism clearly hadn't reached this part of the city. We continued going until a long-forgotten overgrown cemetery stood in front of us. The writing on the graves was largely in Eastern Arabic. Having spent 15 days in Iraq we'd learned to recognise some numbers, so we were able to decipher a few of the dates. Most were centuries old.

We finished our stroll an hour or so later, when the sun came out and turned the mild pleasant morning into a furnace.

While walking through Mardin, we noticed that there were many abandoned houses. At some point an alternative idea for accommodation popped in our minds; maybe squatting could be an option. Well, to be honest, it was more Rebecca's mind than mine. I was looking forward to a shower and some additional comforts, but certainly didn't fancy paying through the nose for this short-lived pleasure. Reluctantly, I decided to go along with her squatting idea.

Finding the right place wasn't too hard. There were a few options, including an abandoned building with a rooftop view. In the end we opted for some old dwellings running one level below the main street. Most of it wasn't suitable for living, except this one room, which was ready for us to move in. Someone had worked hard to make this place feel homely.

In the corner of the room laid an old sofa. Right in front of it was an old TV. There was no electricity there, so it sat there purely for decoration. My only worry was that somebody was still living in this "apartment" and would return at some point and unexpectedly find us there. Before moving in we monitored the place at different times throughout the day; nothing indicated that it was being used.

We returned in the evening after the sun had set. Placing our own mats on the floor, we swiftly arranged our sleeping space and got ready for some shuteye. I wish I could say that I slept like a log, but once the lights were off, I started imagining the worst. And the worst that my mind could come up with was rats. I realised that the room could be an ideal hiding place for them. It was like an obsessive thought I couldn't get out of my mind. Remember the bears? Well it was like that all over again, but with rats this time. Every little sound I heard, I'd turn the torch on and look for signs of rodents. I couldn't wait for the night to pass.

After my sleepless night it was definitely time to find a hotel room. I needed to wash that unpleasant memory off my skin. Probably, over time I could have got used to squatting, but this particular experience wasn't something I would want to repeat any time soon. Rebecca, on the other hand, slept like a baby. As far as saving money on accommodation goes, I prefer to stay in a tent.

Cheap thrills

We had a lot of fun making our way up through Eastern Turkey back to Georgia. Crossing the border, felt like returning home. We even spent a couple of nights in our old Batumi apartment. Though we felt very much connected to this place, we knew it was time to move on, to see other parts of Georgia and to finally start making our way up to enter Russia.

Our next destination was Mestia in the Caucasus Mountains. The plan was to stay there for the bigger part of the summer, if we could find the right place for the right price.

Mestia is one of the most popular tourist destinations in the country. It's a small town in the heart of the mountainous Svanetia region, known for its defensive stone towers, built to protect families against outside dangers. People who live there are said to be fearless hardy fighters, toughened by the endless attacks from invading armies; archetypal highland warriors.

Mestia is a haven for nature lovers. Despite the rapidly-growing number of visitors, nature is still unspoiled and gives plenty of opportunities to explore the wilderness. The region is also popular with motorcyclists, and we hoped to meet some like-minded bikers during our stay.

We hung around in the area for a couple of days and would have stayed much longer, but unfortunately the internet in the village was almost non-existent. We needed a reliable internet connection two days a week, because we worked online to keep our travel kitty topped up. We decided to find somewhere to stay in a nearby city and to visit the mountains every opportunity we could.

The nearest city happened to be Zugdidi. It was a medium size city, with an exceptionally limited choice of accommodation. There was a shabby, overpriced hotel, a boutique guesthouse that was way over our budget, and a small hostel, unimaginatively named The Zugdidi Hostel. We made enquires and tried to negotiate a better long-term deal in each of the places. The hostel was our top choice; it seemed decent enough and the price per night wasn't bad. The owners, a Georgian couple, were really friendly, but we weren't so keen on spending a large amount of time sleeping in an 8-bed dorm with no space or peace and quiet for ourselves. Plus the price wasn't the bargain we were looking for, for a long-term stay.

We really weren't convinced Zugdidi was for us and we'd have probably left if it wasn't for Rebecca's stroke of genius; she asked if we could camp in the garden. We hit the jackpot; the price was just a fraction of what we'd have paid for a single dorm bed. It was such a good deal that initially we weren't sure whether we'd misunderstood and whether the given price was per person or for the two of us. It didn't really matter, though, because it was a bargain either way.

When we went to pay a few days later, it was confirmed that we hadn't been mistaken: the price was what we'd thought. It was less than £1 per night! For that we had our own garden space, 24/7 Wi-Fi, access to showers, toilets and the kitchen area, a safe off-road gated space for our motorcycle and complementary tea. The garden was away from the main house, giving us privacy and peace when we wanted it. The hostel also proved to be really quiet, guests who did come to stay, tended to be Russian or Polish families with children, who all spent their days out on excursions.

Nearby there was a large bazaar where we shopped for food, and if we were feeling lazy and didn't want to cook, there were a few really nice inexpensive restaurants, and a couple of small places selling tasty local snacks. It was such a good deal that we decided to stay there for at least a month, possibly longer.

My background in project management taught me that the client always wants the end result finished quickly, to be of good quality and at a low price, but in reality it's only possible to have any two of these characteristics, never all three. It's exactly the same with motorcycle travels; you simply can't have it all, but you can find a compromise that suits you. Having a small budget, ours had to be cheap. But cheap doesn't have to mean bad, as long as your trip's slow, slow enough for you to negotiate prices of accommodation and shop where locals shop for their food and other supplies.

Besides being a good base, Zugdidi itself didn't offer many attractions. The heart of the city was its Botanical Gardens. The grounds were well cared for and free for everyone to enjoy, so it was always busy with people of all ages. It was a pleasant place to stroll, enjoy an ice-cream or a pack of shelled sunflower seeds; a popular treat sold by older ladies throughout the gardens. We'd spend hours there, people watching and planning our next escapade. Every few days we'd pack our stuff and leave the city to explore a new corner of the region.

For our first trip, we chose to return to Mestia. We knew what to expect because we'd already done the trip once before; the drive was almost effortless; short and easy, despite the ever-present cows, overzealous dogs pouncing at us, or occasional pig strolling across the road.

In Mestia we wild camped away from the town. The landscape was breathtaking and nature at its best; untouched. We hiked to the bottom of the glacier and, as expected, met only a small handful of other tourists during the whole day. It was a hiker's paradise, but even though this is one of Georgia's 'main tourist highlights', numbers are small when compared to other European travel destinations. When we were there, Georgia was still very much a choice destination for the more adventurous traveller.

Before going back to the hostel we camped one more night on route to Zugdidi. This time we pitched our tent on the outskirts of a small village. The next morning we were woken up by voices outside the tent. It seemed that somebody had come to visit us. Still half asleep, I unzipped the front door and poked my head out. Two older guys greeted me with smiles and large reused Coca-Cola bottles filled to the brim with some kind of alcohol. It seemed they'd already had their first bottles that morning. The two bottles they'd brought with them were filled with home-made wine to welcome their guests and the new day.

Men in Georgia love their wine (and chacha). During our time in the country we received countless offers to join locals for a drink. Most times the fact that I was driving a motorcycle wasn't a good enough excuse to abstain, like on this occasion.

Neither Rebecca nor I fancied getting drunk for breakfast, certainly not at 7 o'clock in the morning, so we politely refused the offer. That didn't deter these two guys from enjoying their second liquid breakfast. The bottles were soon empty and with a newfound dollop of Dutch courage, they both pulled out their phones and asked to have their picture taken with us and the motorcycle. We suspected it was more the motorbike that they wanted in their pictures. So while they posed for each, we had time and space to pack. When we were done, we said our goodbyes and jumped on the bike to make our way back to our little garden retreat.

The hostel had become our new home and a place to rest. Marika, the manager, was the heart and soul of the place. She was an outspoken advocate for the Samegrelo region, always keen to share her knowledge and help people plan their escapades. Her enthusiasm and love for the region was infectious.

Samegrelo is one of the least known regions of Georgia, underfunded by the government and unappreciated by unknowing tourists, yet it's truly rich and beautiful in its offerings. One day, armed with detailed directions from Marika, we departed in search of a hidden paradise she'd told us about; a place of pristine forests, high mountains and crystal clear waterfalls. She said we'd need to trek for two days to get there.

To prepare ourselves we bought enough food to last a few days. Then we drove past all the villages and arrived at a small monastery on a hillside; it was the landmark that indicated the start of our route. Before leaving the motorcycle with the monks, we went to the monastery to let somebody know about our plans. When we knocked the door the monks were just about to start their lunch and so invited us to share the meal. The food was delicious. It probably tasted better knowing that we were going to be on rations for the following few days. They were fun to be around; good natured, humorous and knowledgeable. Besides the food, they also gave us some useful tips about the area we were about to explore.

After the lunch was over, I picked up our duffle bag and off we went. We'd packed the bare minimum (our tent, two sleeping bags, our stove, food and water), which doesn't sound like much, but it made for a pretty uncomfortable walk, especially when going for miles on end. At some point the weight became too much to bear and we decided to set up camp earlier than planned. By pure luck we found a fantastic spot, located by the side of a crystal-clear mountain stream, with a small waterfall on the opposite side. The place was surrounded by bushy trees, giving us perfect privacy. It was the best camping spot we'd ever had.

The next morning, knowing that there probably wasn't a living soul for miles around us, we had an icy shower under the waterfall. Afterwards we decided to make this place our base, spend the day speed-hiking and come back in the evening. It was a better plan than lugging our heavy bag around. Just to be on the safe side, we packed our tent and hid everything in the bushes.

Lightweight, we set off to explore the valley. The path was interwoven with a shallow river and every few minutes we had to take off our shoes to make a crossing. Sometimes it wasn't even worth putting them back on because the only way forward was to cross the same river just a few minutes later. We were making very slow progress, but loved the experience and the challenges that the landscape was throwing at us. It was a fun-packed day of adventure.

A good few hours into our walk, to our utter disbelief, a lorry appeared. Driving through this valley required real talent, even inside this old Soviet lorry with wheels taller than most cars. In fact I don't think I would have believed it possible, if I hadn't seen it with my own eyes.

We'd never hitchhiked on top of a Soviet truck and thought it was time to do so. We'd been making little progress walking anyway, so hitching a ride seemed like our only chance to get deeper into the valley. We stuck our thumbs out and were soon invited to climb onboard. To say that it was a bumpy ride would be an understatement; it was like being thrown around in a tumble dryer.

Half an hour later, past some ten river crossings and many miles further down the valley we came to a fork in the road. We could continue on foot along the river or stay in the lorry and be taken out of the valley. It seemed better to jump off and follow the river, so that's what we did.

The valley soon turned into a narrow gorge flooded with water, waist deep. After some consideration, we decided to take our clothes off and continue through this natural shallow lake. We walked and swam for as long as we could, until it started to rain. Afraid that the water level could suddenly rise and trap us in the current, we turned back. Though it wasn't the place that Marika had sent us to, we were happy that we'd found this spot. It felt like we were real adventures, in some tiny unexplored corner of the planet.

The next day we went for an even longer hike, this time up the mountain. We found more waterfalls, came across wild horses and enjoyed spectacular views. Throughout the entire day we didn't meet or see a single person. After two nights in the wild, we'd run out of food and so went reluctantly back to civilisation.

Throughout the summer we continued exploring the region using Zugdidi Hostel as our base. We stayed for almost two months, and probably would have stayed longer, but it was already mid-summer and we wanted to explore more of the country before once again becoming winter-bound.

Moving east

Next on our radar was the capital of Georgia, Tbilisi. Once again, using AirBnB, Rebecca found us a cheap guesthouse room to rent on a month-to-month basis. It had a safe space for our motorcycle and was conveniently located near a large bazaar; and a metro station from where we could easily travel to the centre (a single journey was something like £0.20).

We found Tbilisi to be a vibrant and likable city. It also seemed trendier than other parts of Georgia. We were keen to make the most of our time there.

Every other weekend, we'd jump on the motorcycle and hit the road. Our first destination was David Gareja, a large well-known monastery complex, situated less than sixty miles south-east of Tbilisi. The monastery is located near the Azerbaijani boarder, in an isolated corner of Georgia. Beyond the only access road, sits a wide strip of no-man's land, creating an invisible divide between the two countries.

The land was largely uninhabited, probably due to the winds which would ever-so-often ferociously blow through the hills, making it extremely hard for even the smallest of nature to withstand it, let alone thrive. Yet somehow this harsh and forbidding landscape had once attracted a group of Assyrian monks, willing to work extremely hard to construct the monastery in this place. The complex, though built in the 6th century, remained in good condition. It includes hundreds of small cells, churches, and living quarters hollowed out of the rock face.

After seeing the monastery, we continued further east, to Signage, one of the smallest towns in Georgia, renowned for its charm and good wine.

The town is situated on a steep hill, overlooking a picturesque landscape. It's a touristy place with plenty of hotels, restaurants and street vendors selling all sorts of things, anything from hand-made woollen socks to cheap mass produced toys from China. We spent a couple of hours strolling around and once we'd had enough, we jumped on the bike and left for an exploration around the outside of town.

Soon I found myself away from the main roads, following some narrow dirt track on a hillside. There was a church in the distance across the valley and I decided to head there. I managed to find a path that looked like it would get us there. It was very steep and unfortunately, it quickly turned into a pile of loose stones; continuing as slowly as was possible, I was hopeful that it would be a short drive. Very soon, I began to regret my decision; the suspension on my bike was being massacred and it didn't seem that we were getting any closer to the church.

It took us at least another half an hour to reach the bottom of the valley. Both, the front and back brakes were sizzling. Luckily, the stones soon turned into a dirt path once again, which made it much easier to continue. We whizzed up the other side of the mountain, cooling the bike and ourselves. There was no church at the top, but the panoramic view more than compensated for it. We decided to stay there overnight.

As we started setting up the tent, I thought of something unusual that had happened earlier that day; on three, maybe four separate occasions we were warned about snakes. That had never happened to us in Georgia before, but we decided to take extra care. Despite the heat, we kept our motorcycle boots on and stomped a lot everywhere we went in the grass. Not to kill anything below our feet, but to send warning vibrations to any unwelcome guests slithering around nearby.

Just before the sun set, a shepherd with a flock of sheep came our way. We happened to be camping on his route. He was probably in his seventies and had a friendly smile. One of the first things he said to us was to watch out for snakes. Before continuing, he invited us to his nearby place. I happily agreed to go along, while Rebecca decided to stay in the tent.

His place was just a small wooden shack. Inside there was a makeshift bed, one chair and a small drawer to keep his personal things clean. There was no electricity, nor running water. He lit a candle and asked me to sit on his bed. Then, he took out some dry cheese and chacha (Georgian grape pomace brandy, which tastes very much like vodka). It was a good ice-breaker; after a couple of shots our conversation became easier and livelier. I learned about his time in the army, about his family and about the sheep. The old man liked talking and I'm sure he appreciated having some company.

I knew we both needed to get up early the next day, so I said good night and headed back to Rebecca. It was pitch-black outside when I was leaving. Even with my head-torch, I'd stand no chance spotting snakes. All I could do was to make as much noise as possible. Being quite tipsy, I happily stomped and sang my way back to the tent. It didn't matter that snakes are deaf. In fact it was probably better for them that they couldn't hear me sing.

The end of biking season

We spent the whole biking season driving around Georgia and getting to know the country.

In autumn our friends were getting married and we didn't want to miss their special day. It meant that we had to fly back to the UK and arrange our journey around their wedding date. And even though we already wanted to begin our Russian adventure, it was more convenient to stay in Georgia until the wedding, and consequently until spring. Entering Russia just before winter wouldn't make sense. Our plans were made for us.

Through a local friend, we found someone who was willing to store our motorcycle, an American called Denis. He and his family had been living in Tbilisi for years. They had their own house on the outskirts of the city.

We arrived at their place a couple of days before our flight and were relieved to find that there was plenty of secure space for our machine, in a garage next to his own motorcycles. Denis had an old Russian Dnepr with a side basket and a couple of smaller dirt bikes. He ran a small church in Tbilisi and talked a lot about his religion and god. At one point we thought he might try to convert us, but that wasn't his aim, he was just passionate about his work. He seemed like a good trustworthy guy, and we left knowing our bike would be in safe hands.

Being back in Europe was a welcomed break. It was nice to see our friends and family. While in the UK we also sorted our Russian visas. They were due to start in March 2015.

Our return flight was scheduled for late October. We were heading back to Georgia to wait out the winter. Truthfully, we didn't look forward to spending the entire winter in one place, but the cost of living in Georgia was cheaper than in any other place we'd been. One day before the departure, I received an email from the airline. They'd rescheduled the flight and as a result we had two choices: to accept the change or to have a full refund. Nothing like this had ever happened to us before, so we thought hard about our options and decided that it was an opportunity. So instead of spending the whole winter in Georgia, we decided to take the refund and fly to sunny Asia. We contacted Denis and as expected, he didn't mind looking after our bike for an additional few months. One quick decision and we put our motorcycle journey on hold and flew to Thailand.

In Asia we spent the next four months visiting various countries. We travelled mainly by train or bus, only occasionally renting a scooter. We missed our motorcycle at times, but not the cold. There was plenty to keep us busy in Asia and we enjoyed every second of those four months.

Forks and tripe

In February we returned to Georgia. It was still cold, but the weather was slowly improving. We had over a month before our planned entry to Russia, which was plenty of time to get all the bike maintenance done.

To ensure that all went smoothly, before getting back to Georgia, I'd arranged to see a local bike mechanic.

A few days after our arrival in Tbilisi I collected the motorcycle from Denis's house. I'd left the year before thinking it would only be for a couple of weeks, but it ended up being more than 4 months. The bike wasn't prepped for such a long period of idleness. I was expecting some difficulty starting it and when I got there I found the battery completely dead. This was expected, so I'd come with a new one in hand. Even with the new battery, cleaned spark plugs and fresh petrol, the engine refused to cooperate. It took a while, but with some persistence, and help from Denis, the bike finally started. When I was leaving, I realised that the front suspension was in terrible condition. It was bad before, but now it was almost impossible to drive.

From Denis's I went straight to the mechanic; a young boy called Nika, whom I found through Horizons Unlimited. He had his own garage where he did odd jobs for cash. It was either him or the local KTM garage, reported by many to overcharge foreigners. Besides the matter of cost, I wanted to be involved in the work and Nika didn't mind.

There were two main things I wanted him to help me with; changing the fork oil along with all the seals, and also fitting new tyres. Everything else I was happy to do on my own with my travelling set of tools.

We met at the agreed location, outside the metro station. I suppose my first impression of him wasn't the best as he showed up half an hour late and was acting a little bit strangely. I soon realised that it was just his way; a bit eccentric. He was around my age, very chatty and a bit bossy at times. He was a good guy, though; it was easy to see kindness underneath that odd facade. The most important thing was that he seemed to know his way around motorcycles.

During our first meeting we agreed to start working early the next day. In the morning I arrived early. Nika arrived late, again. Without much delay we began working. The first fork was done within a couple of hours. It was easy enough to work together, despite his occasional short temper. I appreciated that he took time to involve me in every step along the way.

In the afternoon I offered to take us for lunch. Nika happily recommended a nearby diner. When it came to ordering, my companion suggested that I must try this "delicious Georgian dish". I'm not fussy about food, but on this occasion I was horrified and disgusted by the look and smell of what was put in front of me; I'd ended up with a huge bowl of tripe, the one dish that I can't stomach (pun intended). I tried eating it, but it was impossible; the dish stank. Nika kept repeating that I had to finish it. At first I thought he was winding me up, but after a while I realised that he was seriously annoyed. He became like an impatient parent. In the end I managed to convince him that I should take this "delicious dish" for Rebecca to try, though in reality I knew she wouldn't touch it either. What I actually intended to do was to chuck it in the first bin I saw. Later that day, after the work in the garage was done, and away from Nika's scolding looks, I fed it to some stray dogs. They didn't mind the smell at all and wolfed the whole lot down ravenously.

On the second day, we put everything back together and tested the forks. I was pleased with the result. The next task was to replace the rear tyre. I specifically wanted to do it manually, just in case one day I'd get stuck with a flat with nobody else to rely on but myself. It was important for me to learn. Nika seemed confident that we could do it. And indeed, it was easy going at first; the old tyre came off in a jiffy.

The new tyre, which I brought from the UK, was ready to be put on the bike. It took some muscle to force the first edge of the tyre over the rim, but some resistance was expected. At this point I was actually surprised to find that changing the tyre was so easy. A few more steps and a bit more elbow grease and we'd be done, or so I thought. After carefully aligning the inner tube inside the tyre, it was time for the final step; forcing the other edge of the tyre over the rim, which quickly proved to be the hardest part.

We hit a brick wall. Armed with as many tyre irons as we could possibly handle, we continued wrestling with it, but it felt almost as if the tyre was too small. On top of that Nika was getting real mad, and the communication between us suffered as a consequence. Eventually he dropped his tools to the floor and screamed a litany of Georgian swearwords. After venting his anger, he explained that one of the irons had punctured a large hole in the inner tube. It was time to accept defeat; we couldn't do it without help. Luckily I had a spare tube. It had been sitting at the bottom of my luggage for almost two years, waiting for a moment like this one. I was actually glad I could finally use it. All we needed now was a tyre fitting shop.

Nika knew a nearby garage where we could get the job done. When we got there, I waited by the gate while he went inside to check the price. He came back out a minute later in a right strop; before he left I'd heard him angrily shout something at the owner, who'd responded in a similar tone. Instead of dropping it, Nika went back for a full blown argument. I was pretty sure they'd end up fighting, but fortunately the owner gave in to his lunacy. Only then Nika was able to walk away, bearing a triumphant smile on his face. My mechanic had some serious anger management issues, but I needed his help to finish the job.

After calming down a bit, he tried to explain the reason for his anger: apparently the garage owner wanted more money than usual; an increase that was unacceptable. Talking about it made him angry once again. When he told me how much the guy wanted to charge him, I almost lost it myself. The increase was nothing, less than I would spend on a couple of doughnuts. Even with the increase, the price would have been just a fraction of what I'd pay back home. I had to stop myself from saying something. After all, he was saving my money (though I don't think that's what drove his behaviour). Anyway, it was too late to ponder about it; the damage had been done and we had to move on.

The other garage that Nika knew of was miles away. Getting a taxi was out of the question for him. It was too expensive and he was adamant about it (in comparison to Western countries, taxis in Georgia are very cheap). Instead, we had to take two busses and then walk for another ten minutes to get there. With the motorcycle wheel in my hand and an emotionally unstable mechanic at my side, it wasn't fun. Once there, we were told that basically we'd come for nothing. They didn't have the right equipment to service motorcycle tyres and refused to even touch it.

We had to call it a day. On our way back to the garage, I insisted on getting a taxi. Nika agreed very reluctantly, but only under the condition that we pay the right price, his price. In Georgia taxis don't have a meter so you either pay a customary price or agree it with the driver before taking off. I trusted that he knew what he was talking about, which was my mistake. Within twenty minutes only three taxis stopped and he angrily sent them all away. He was unreasonable, unable to compromise. I took the initiative with the next driver that stopped and, sure enough, I got us a ride back to the garage for a sensible price.

I returned early the next day to continue our venture. It was the third day together and frankly speaking we were getting tired of each other. We were just too different to gel. I was only hoping that the tyre problem would be solved quickly this time and we'd both be able to return to our own worlds.

In order to find somebody who could help us with the tyre, we had to head to the Eliava Bazaar, located on the opposite side of the city. The Eliava is a vast open-air market selling everything from building materials, tools and machinery, to second-hand car parts and army surplus - much of it Russian-made, remnants harking back to Soviet days. Importantly for us, there was a street specialising in vehicle mechanics.

The first place we approached sent us away. Without the right tools, they didn't want to risk damaging the rim. We continued searching and after visiting probably another dozen places, we finally found someone willing to help us. It was a small backstreet garage, run by some young boys. I wasn't filled with confidence, but neither did I have a choice.

I handed over my tyre to one of the boys but stayed vigilant to what was happening. He seemed a bit unsure about what to do next, so I wanted to make sure that he knew his stuff. I couldn't risk him damaging my wheel, tube or tyre. Wanting to figure out what was happening, I asked Nika to act as my translator. But instead of helping me, you guessed it, he just got angry and basically told me to be quiet. I'd had enough; this time I got angry and gave him a proper earful. I told the young boy to stop working on my tyre and was about to walk away. Luckily the other lad came and took over the work. I could see right away that he knew exactly what to do. He was confident and quick, so I relaxed a bit. Nika and I waited, avoiding each other's eyes, but the air could have been cut with a knife. The job was finished within minutes.

After leaving the place, I apologised to Nika for getting angry, but he wasn't interested. I didn't mind as I was happy with the silent treatment. This ordeal was over; we just had to return to the garage. To shorten the journey, I once again got us a taxi.

We never agreed on the exact payment for his work, though I had a pretty good idea how much it should cost. I was just hoping that after our quarrel I wouldn't end up in yet another uncomfortable situation.

Back in his garage I asked about the payment, but instead of telling me the price, he suggested that I give "whatever I think is right". That's exactly what I did, and luckily he was happy with it. On top of that, I gave him my old tyre, which still had plenty of thread on it. This put an even bigger smile on his face and I was his friend again. It was a good ending for our short encounter.

When travelling, it's necessary to rely on other people, sometimes the strangest of people.

Our half-baked trip to Armenia

To properly road-test the bike we planned a short trip to Armenia; we'd wanted to go for a while but always found some other place to explore first. Finally it was time to visit this enigmatic country about which we'd heard a lot. Like with most countries, the stories were never consistent, often contradictory. Some travellers loved it for its nature and national parks, while others reported poverty and general unhappiness. The only piece of information that everyone seemed to agree on was the fact that in Armenia almost everyone wears black. We believed Georgians were similar in that respect, especially older generations.

Anyway, economically, Armenia is way behind its neighbour. Though an independent country since 1991, in many ways it still has to rely on Russia. This is due to its unfortunate location between oil-rich Azerbaijan and power-hungry Turkey. Presently Armenia constitutes only one-tenth of its historical territory.

We arrived at the boarder around midday. Leaving Georgia was hassle-free, as always. Entering Armenia was much more complicated. On the first checkpoint, one of the officers inspected the bike and issued an entry stamp. Next we had to go to the office to process temporary import documents for the motorcycle.

We parked the bike in the designated area in front of the building and entered a small office. There was only one room, but about six different counters with six long queues.

Most people were truckers who knew exactly what to do. Rebecca and I, on the other hand, were lost. I tried asking a couple of people, but my Russian wasn't good enough to understand the answers and, besides, everyone was busy with their own paperwork. Eventually someone pointed us in the right direction. After a lengthy wait in a queue, I made my way to the desk. With a cigarette hanging out of the corner of his mouth and boredom in his eyes, the middle-aged official looked up at me and, with his nicotine-stained finger, pointed at the price list.

I remember being surprised. We definitely didn't expect the price to be that high, even more than what we'd paid to enter Turkey. We hesitated. Our indecisiveness was met with the official's scolding look; a mix between bureaucratic impatience and his personal hostile indifference. Feeling a bit of pressure from those waiting behind us, we left the building to think about our next step. We really wanted to visit Armenia, but didn't want to be paying so much for a short weekend trip. We decided, partly thanks to the atmosphere at the crossing, that we wouldn't be entering Armenia that day.

As we were getting ready to drive away, we had second thoughts. It came to us that it was probably our once-in-a-lifetime opportunity to visit Armenia on a motorcycle, and regardless of the cost, it would be a shame to miss it. We changed our minds once again and went back to the office.

After another long wait in a queue, we faced the same unwelcoming official. I'd recently learned the word "discount" in Russian and thought it was good time to use it. I was right; the official and the truckers around burst out laughing. Though no discount was offered, I managed to lift the mood for a moment. I filled in the form and paid the fee. Then unexpectedly we were told to pay more, some extra 20% on top of what we'd already paid. That was the final straw; we instantly decided to leave Armenia, before we'd even really entered. The official got really angry when I asked for the money back. I didn't think he would, but after a few uncomfortable minutes he agreed to refund us.

Still, our visit to Armenia wasn't over yet. Our passports had already been stamped, including the vehicle stamp. Every vehicle leaving the country must show temporary import documents, which we didn't have. The border control didn't want to let us out without it and insisted that we pay. That was their protocol and it was futile to explain that we hadn't actually entered the country. In the end I decided to lie, saying that we didn't have enough money and in the end they let us out. After one hour in no-man's land, our Armenian trip came to an end.

As we were driving away Rebecca asked that we not mention this failed adventure to anyone. I agreed.

In the war zone

Before going to Russia, we had to once again visit Zugdidi Hostel, where we'd left some of our clothes and gear the previous year.

There was one main road connecting the capital city with the west coast; the road I dreaded like the plague. To avoid it, I studied Google maps for alternatives. A detour through small villages and country roads seemed possible. Armed with a small hand-drawn map, we hit the road.

The detour was very enjoyable; it led us through some rustic villages and the Georgian countryside. We continued peacefully until in one of the villages some guy stopped his car in front of us and waved us down. I got closer to see what it was about. The guy was in his fifties and was driving a Soviet car even older than he was. His unshaved face and red eyes made us feel suspicious when he claimed to be a policeman. We ignored his request to stop, and drove on. A little further down the road we entered a small village and quickly forgot about the self-proclaimed policeman. I pulled over at the dusty petrol station. Besides filling up the tank and getting some rest, I wanted to make sure that we were heading in the right direction.

Before we'd even had a chance to get off the bike, a small group of Georgian soldiers with guns surrounded us. It wasn't long before our policeman friend showed up. He quickly took control of the situation, proving that he was in fact a real member of the force.

We instantly understood that something wasn't right. We weren't supposed to be there. Unknowingly, we'd entered South Ossetia, a highly volatile conflict zone. Apparently we'd driven straight past a manned blockade. The region is still officially a part of Georgia, but largely occupied by the Russian military. Even the EU Monitoring mission is not allowed to enter.

The strangest thing is that I didn't even get lost; my directions were good and took us exactly where I'd wanted to go. I simply hadn't noticed the faint dotted lines when I was planning the route on the map.

It was a potentially serious situation, though we didn't realise it at the time. The soldiers could have easily arrested us with no questions asked. Luckily they just wanted to know what we were doing there. We stayed calm and answered all the questions, honestly. Once they saw that we weren't spies, but clueless tourists who weren't very good with maps or avoiding conflict zones, they let us free, ordering us to leave the area immediately. We did as told without resistance. On our way out of South Ossetia, we met the soldiers that were supposed to be standing guard at the blockade we'd driven straight through. They seemed surprised to see us. We suspected they must have been on a break when we managed to get past them. We could see a deck of cards and empty glass bottles on a table in their shack-like base.

Our new route wasn't anywhere near as interesting, but it wasn't free from trouble either, just a different kind of trouble this time. Not long after leaving South Ossetia, the motorcycle broke down. I managed to push it to the nearby petrol station to investigate the problem. The petrol was streaming down from the engine. I followed the leak and noticed that one of the fuel pipes had came loose. I spent the next hour trying to reattach it without taking the bike apart. Somehow I managed it, but the bike still wouldn't start. I had no idea what to do next. I was very fortunate because a couple of Czech bikers showed up at the petrol station. Seeing that I was in trouble, they offered to help. Their suspicion was that the carburettor had been flooded and needed cleaning. Together we pulled the bike apart and cleaned and dried everything. It took us a couple of hours to put it back together. After we were done, it seemed to be running as before.

Later, en-route to Zugdidi, I realised that something still wasn't right. One problem was with the choke; it was completely misadjusted, way too high most of the time. It took me two days to bring the revving down to a normal level. The cable itself had pulled off, so once adjusted, the choke was stuck there.

Another problem I was experiencing was to do with the reserve switch. For some reason, unknown to me, the bike behaved as though it had run out of petrol even though there was still plenty left in the tank. The reserve switch was in manual, so I had to do it quickly each time I'd lose power. And it was impossible to predict when it would happen; sometimes it would be after 100 miles, other times after 150, whereas before it would always be almost exactly after 200 miles.

Though this unexpected cutting off of my fuel supply was somewhat dangerous, I quickly got used to the inconvenience and let it be as it was. Besides, we were about to leave for the Russian border, and I didn't think the problem was serious enough to postpone our big plans. It was a mistake, but I wouldn't know it until getting to Siberia.

Crushed pride

Our long-awaited day of leaving for Russia had finally arrived. But before crossing the border, there was one more place we wanted to visit; the Kazbegi district, which is probably the most beautiful part of the country, and believe me there are plenty to choose from in Georgia. Its main town is Stepantsminda, colloquially called Kazbegi. Scenically located amongst the Greater Caucasus Mountains, the city was slowly becoming a tourist magnet.

That's where we met Tom, a solo Turkish motorcyclist on his way to Mongolia. We drove up to the iconic Georgian church, located on a nearby mountain. We knew that this place was often used by hikers and mountaineers as a base camp.

The road leading to the church wasn't for the fainthearted; it was steep and covered in a mass of large stones. It reminded me of a dry river bed. Tourists would either walk up or pay a skilled 4x4 taxi driver to get them to the top. Normal cars or inexperienced drivers stood no chance. I figured that we should somehow make it on our motorcycles.

The first twenty yards proved me wrong. On just this short stretch of the road (if I could call it a road), our Turkish friend dropped his bike three times. He was failing miserably and getting more peeved by the second. I wasn't exactly skilled at it either, but the height of his bike was his main problem. He simply couldn't properly reach the ground with his feet so had no help in keeping his balance. At his parking lot speed, as soon as his balance was lost it meant him and his bike hitting the ground with a thud.

The situation was embarrassing for him. It became even worse when 4x4s started zipping down the same narrow path, giving us no choice but to move out of the way. In his distress he dropped the bike again, twice, making him even more frustrated. Finally he asked me to bring his bike safely back down. Needless to say, his pride was in tatters.

Once down, I suggested a new destination. There was a picturesque valley nearby, where I was sure we could find a decent spot to camp.

We reached the valley within minutes. There were plenty of camping spaces right there, but we decided to continue, searching for something a bit more special. Soon the road turned into a dirt path with streams to cross and shallow pools of water to navigate through. He tagged slowly behind us, probably choosing to stay on the safe side. Eventually we found a spot we wanted to stop at, but to get there we had to drive down a steep, rocky path, similar to the one leading up to the church. Not wanting to fall again, he handed his bike over to me; yet another blow to his pride.

Our camping spot was idyllic. Situated deep in the valley, we were surrounded by vast rugged mountains with white peaks glowing at the top in the slowly setting sun. A freezing cold mountain river was gushing just a few yards away from us. There was absolutely nobody else around, just us and nature. Once it had become dark, millions of stars appeared in the sky. The place was truly magical, better than any hotel.

After a good night's sleep, we left the site. Once more I helped Tom to get his bike back on the road. On this occasion it felt quite natural, as if it had already become a part of our daily routine.

Instead of driving back to town, we decided to continue climbing up the path, to see where it would take us. We began a steady climb up the valley. The road surface was pretty bad, with deep holes and occasional passageways carved out by mountain streams. But the further we ascended, the better the view and deeper the valley below us. We were getting really high and it was breathtaking (beautiful and scary at the same time). Not wanting to tempt our luck, I drove as far away from the drop as possible.

We slowly made it to the top, where we found a small mountain village. We parked our bikes where the road ended and continued to explore the area on foot.

We strolled for miles following a small river. The area was lush, clean and unspoiled. We continued walking until a mountain ranger on horseback showed up. Apparently we'd got too close to the Russian border and were told to turn around.

We returned to the bikes and began heading back to town for breakfast. Rebecca and I drove first, our new companion followed not far behind. As before, I was keeping away from the drop, staying on the safe side (or so I thought).

Suddenly the peaceful morning ended with a loud bang. I lost control of the bike and veered towards the drop. Everything happened in a split second, but I recall knowing that our fall was inevitable.

What happened next was beyond any conscious decision-making on my part, but I like to think that somehow I chose to drop the bike to the ground, instead of allowing it to drive us into the depths of the valley below. We landed right on the edge, the front wheel hanging over, threatening to pull the bike down with us on it, or flying beside it!

We were pretty fortunate in our misfortune; our accident could have been fatal. Despite being visibly shaken, physically we were both unharmed. Emotionally though, we were shell-shocked, speechless. The crash hit me like a hammer.

Our fellow biker having witnessed everything from behind, immediately got off his machine and rushed towards us, laughing, which was the last thing we needed at that point. He seemed to get a kick out of our accident; it really didn't seem to be a nervous reaction. He joked that he'd thought he'd have to send news to our parents that we were goners. In a twisted way, our own setback seemed to have restored his sense of dignity. I'm not sure he was aware of it, but he just couldn't stop grinning.

Once the adrenaline rush had finished, I picked the bike up and dusted off our panniers. We jumped back on the bike as soon as I felt calm and focussed enough to drive again. We parted ways with our Turkish companion soon after leaving the valley.

Starting a new chapter

We spent the rest of the day peacefully, wandering about the town, sipping coffee and chatting with other tourists. When evening came, we decided to head towards the Russian border and find a place to camp along the famous Georgian Military Road.

We found a nice piece of ground with a scenic mountain view just outside the town. It has to be said that during our stay in Georgia, we were blessed with many such spectacular spots. When it came to wild camping, Georgia was a delight. We hoped Russia would have similar camping spots to offer.

As planned, the next day we woke up early and arrived at the border before it opened. There was already a huge line of drivers waiting to go through, mainly heavy goods vehicles. We dashed past them and reached the frontier. Though slightly anxious, we were excited about moving on.

It was a sunny morning and a good day to start a new chapter; driving through mighty Russia.

- The end -

We'd appreciate if you could give us a **review on Amazon.**
Thanks you

Also, you can visit us at **www.facebook.com/nomadsatheart/**

You can also subscribe to our mailing list to hear about our latest books.

http://www.nomadsatheart.co.uk/mailing-list/

About us

We met in London, in 2005. Rebecca had just finished her university degree and had been living in London for a good few years. I, on the other hand, was relatively new to the UK, having recently dropped out of university back in Poland. I'd figured that Politics wasn't for me, and as many other young people do, I went to London in search of change. And here the story starts, Rebecca and I found ourselves working in the same pub in north London and we hit it off instantly.

There were many things that drew us together, music and our shared love of Pink Floyd was the first, but it was probably the zest for adventure we both shared which sealed the deal. Within the first few months of our relationship, we'd quit our jobs and jumped on a flight to India for three months of backpacking around the country. It was quite an adventure and turned out to be a real test on how much we wanted to be together; the "make or break" trip for us as a couple. Despite some difficulties, cultural shocks and a few very stressful situations, which included some hair-raising bus journeys, we made it through, still together.

We got back to the UK with what you might have heard other travellers call 'the travel bug', but before we could set off on any other major adventures, we needed to organise ourselves. We blue-tacked a big map of the world on a wall of our studio apartment and marked all the places we wanted to visit. We both found jobs and started saving for our next big trip. I quickly grew fed up with low paid jobs and signed up for a degree in Information Systems and Management at LSE (the London School of Economics). This time, having paid for it with my own hard-earned cash, I stuck it out until graduating. In my spare time, which I had very little of, I studied for other IT certificates. Soon the hard work paid off and I got my first IT job working for the London City Council.

Rebecca was also working her butt off. Her love for other cultures and for learning, led her to do a year-long certificate in teaching English as a foreign language. After qualifying she worked hard to develop her skills as an English teacher, and in her spare time she gave private lessons to make more cash to add to our travel fund.

It was a challenging three years, but by the end of it we'd saved enough to leave everything behind again; this time we bought two one-way tickets to South America. The plan was to stay there exploring until our money ran out.

After an amazing four months spent travelling from country to country, we settled down for a bit in Poland. I got a job as an IT Project Manager and Rebecca continued teaching English.

Little did we know that just a few years later, in 2013, we'd sell pretty much everything we owned to embark on a motorcycle adventure of a lifetime.

Having gained some travelling experience over the years, we knew that we wanted more freedom to move around countries. As much as we'd enjoyed "most" of our public transport adventures when abroad, we wanted to break free from this style of travelling and to have more independence. Hitting the road by motorcycle seemed like the ideal solution. It was our ultimate means to freedom. From that point on we've embraced the simple life of permanent but slow travellers. Back in 2013 we became homeless by choice and haven't regretted it for a moment. We feel privileged to live the lifestyle we want and to have the freedom we have. What we value most in life is freedom and we feel blessed not only to have such freedom, but also to share it with each other.

Printed by Amazon Italia Logistica S.r.l.
Torrazza Piemonte (TO), Italy